CLIL Readers

 Audio available

Amazing insects

written by
Amy White

There are a lot of insects in the world. They can live just about anywhere. All insects have six legs and most have two antennae.

Insects also have three body parts: head, thorax and abdomen. If an animal has these parts, then it is an insect for sure!

There are many kinds of insects. Some have strange shapes. The *peanut head leaf bug* has a peanut shaped head.

This is called the *giraffe weevil leaf bug*. It is named after the giraffe because they both have long necks.

Some insects change shape. Do you know what a caterpillar changes into? A butterfly!

A caterpillar changes shape inside the chrysalis. This process is called 'metamorphosis'.

Some insects look like other things. This insect is called a *walking stick* because it looks like a stick.

Can you guess what this insect is called?
It is called a *leaf bug* because it looks like
a leaf.

The leaf bug and the walking stick can hide to protect themselves. Their colour and shape match their surroundings.

Some insects are very big. This is a *giant water bug*. Giant water bugs can be as long as twelve centimetres.

Some insects are so big that they can eat other insects. They can even eat frogs or small fish.

Some insects make homes. For example, bees make hives to live in. They also use the hives to store their honey.

Ants make anthill colonies. Anthills are like cities for ants. Ants live and work together in their anthills.

Scientists found an anthill in Japan that had more than three hundred million ants!

There are so many insects in the world that they cannot even be counted. Insects are everywhere!